MW00593502

Text © 2006 by Monte Farber
Art © 2006 by Amy Zerner

10 9 8 7 6 5 4 3 2

Published by Sterling Publishing Co., Inc.
387 Park Avenue South, New York, NY 10016

Distributed in Canada by Sterling Publishing
c/o Canadian Manda Group, 165 Dufferin Street
Toronto, Ontario, Canada M6K 3H6

Distributed in the United Kingdom by GMC
Distribution Services
Castle Place, 166 High Street, Lewes, East Sussex,
England BN7 1XU

Distributed in Australia by Capricorn Link (Australia)
Pty. Ltd.
P.O. Box 704, Windsor, NSW 2756, Australia

Printed in China
All rights reserved

Sterling ISBN-13: 978-1-4027-4181-4
        ISBN-10: 1-4027-4181-2

For information about custom editions, special sales,
premium and corporate purchases, please contact
Sterling Special Sales Department at 800-805-5489 or
specialsales@sterlingpub.com.

What's Your Sign?

When someone asks you "What's your sign?" you know what that person really means is "What's your astrological sign?" Professional astrologers more often use the phrase "Sun sign," a term reflecting the concept that a person's sign is determined by which of the twelve signs of the zodiac the Sun appeared to be passing through at the moment she was born. The zodiac is the narrow band of sky circling the Earth's equator through which the Sun, the Moon, and the planets appear to move when viewed by us here on Earth.

Astrology's Gift

Astrology, which has been around for thousands of years, is the study of how planetary positions relate to earthly events and people. Its long and rich history has resulted in a wealth of philosophical and psychological wisdom, the basic concepts of which we are going to share with you in the pages of this book. As the Greek philosopher Heracleitus (c. 540–c. 480 BCE) said, "Character is destiny." Who you are—complete with all of your goals, tendencies, habits, virtues, and vices—will

determine how you act and react, thereby creating your life's destiny. Like astrology itself, our Astrology Gems series is designed to help you to better know yourself and those you care about. You will then be better able to use your free will to shape your life to your liking.

Does Astrology Work?

Many people rightly question how astrology can divide humanity into twelve Sun signs and make predictions that can be correct for everyone of the same sign. The simple answer is that it cannot do that—that's newspaper astrology, entertaining but not the real thing. Rather, astrology can help you understand your strengths and weaknesses so that you can better accept yourself as you are and use your strengths to compensate for your weaknesses. Real astrology is designed to help you to become yourself fully.

Remember, virtually all the music in the history of Western music has been composed using variations of the same twelve notes. Similarly, the twelve Sun signs of astrology are basic themes rich with meaning that each of us expresses differently to create and respond to the unique opportunities and challenges of our life.

LIBRA

September 23–October 22

Planet
Venus

Element
Air

Quality
Cardinal

Day
Friday

Season
autumn

Colors
light blue, royal blue, pastels

Plants
orchid, foxglove, eucalyptus

Perfume
vanilla

Gemstones
opal, jade, sapphire, blue topaz

Metal
copper

Personal qualities
Artistic, refined, poised, intelligent,
and tactful

KEYWORDS

We call the following words "keywords" because they can help you unlock the core meaning of the astrological sign of Libra. Each keyword represents issues and ideas that are of supreme importance and prominence in the lives of people born with Libra as their Sun sign. You will usually find that every Libra embodies at least one of these keywords in the way she makes a living:

partnership • union • diplomacy
color sense • sophistication
good taste • yin and yang • law
balance • cooperation • fairness
quality control • detachment
aesthetics • harmonious
good manners • politics • ideas
fence-sitter • romantic • justice
opinions • shopping
fashionista • give peace a chance
moderate • pro and con
mellifluous • idealism • comfort

Libra's Symbolic Meaning

Libra is the only sign whose symbol is not alive, not a human, animal, or fish. Its symbol is the old-fashioned balance scale, a representation of equal measure and justice. The scales of Libra remind us that the time of Libra was when the harvest was weighed and measured against those of other years and other farmers. Public declarations of contractual partnerships were made and fulfilled, as goods were exchanged for their fair market value. But the perfect balance of the Libran scales was also a reminder that the first six warming full Moons of the lunar year had passed and that the challenges of the next six cooling full Moons were to come. Our ancestors knew that a balanced, loving relationship was a truly valuable commodity on cold nights. Only a cooperative family unit could make it through winter's deprivations.

Libra is one of the four Cardinal Sun signs in astrology (the other three are Aries, Cancer, and Capricorn). Cardinal people like to initiate change, as each Cardinal sign represents the beginning of a new season. Consequently, they like to take charge, and they take action to direct and control.

Libra is also one of the three Air signs of astrology (the other two are Gemini and Aquarius). The Air signs are usually connected with communication and the intellect.

The lesson for all Libras to learn is that there is an important reason that their judgment is not as refined, elegant, and accurate as they would like it to be. They have come into this world with the astrological sign Libra because they want to learn how to develop their judgment and become the best competitor for the finer things in life. Libras hate anything they consider not up to their standards and want to be surrounded by only the best. Perhaps this is why Libras are such an interesting mixture of refined judgment and fierce competitiveness.

Libras too often allow themselves to be persuaded to abandon their own judgment and distrust their intuition. The scales that symbolize Libra are an inanimate device intended to indicate the relative weight or value of everything by attaining a position of rest, resolution, and harmony. A scale never brought to a state of equilibrium is almost worthless. Libras have a natural affinity with the unseen, intuitive side of life. With the exceedingly rare and keen perception characteristic of the sign Libra, there is no human attainment beyond their grasp.

Recognizing a Libra

People who exhibit the physical characteristics distinctive of the sign Libra have a fine bone structure and balanced features, a charming smile, a graceful and athletic build, and a clear and very harmonious voice. Libras are likely to have an attractive dimple. It is a Libran habit to spend time deciding what to wear each morning, and he knows how to dress in gentle, subtle colors.

Libra's Typical Behavior and Personality Traits

- ❀ has a hard time making decisions
- ❀ enjoys beautiful art and music
- ❀ is a great conversationalist
- ❀ is interested in the opposite sex
- ❀ knows how to be romantic
- ❀ is amusing and smiles a lot
- ❀ is very idealistic

- ❀ can change his mind often
- ❀ can spend a lot of money on luxury items
- ❀ has good business instincts
- ❀ has good manners
- ❀ is interested in legal matters

What Makes a Libra Tick?

Libras are driven by the desire to bring beauty and harmony to their world and the world at large. They have refined tastes and may actually recoil from things that are ugly, loud, or unpleasant. Other people may misinterpret this attitude as snobbishness, but it is not. For many Libras, vulgarity is an affront.

A Libra may give the impression of being a pushover because of an unwillingness to argue. But under the right set of circumstances he can stand up for himself, despite the unpleasantness that arguing brings.

The Libra
Personality
Expressed Positively

Libras who use their talent for mediating disputes in their daily life are acting out their own innate sense of harmony, and they manage to do this without appearing to be nosy or intrusive. They have a genuine desire for peace and equality in every relationship, and when they are happy these attributes are easily attained and flow through their actions.

On a Positive Note

Libras displaying the positive characteristics associated with their sign also tend to be:

❀ cooperative and trustworthy

❀ excellent companions

❀ refined and artistic

❀ idealistic and romantic

❀ good negotiators

❀ fair-minded

❀ strong believers in good causes

❀ planners

❀ charming and sincere

The Libra Personality
Expressed Negatively

An unhappy or frustrated Libra can be hard to get along with and deliberately quarrelsome. If Libra feels that she is lacking in power, she can do a lot of moping and self-pitying. Also, if Libra doesn't get enough attention, the result is likely to be a lowering of confidence and self-esteem. Libra needs to shine in someone else's eyes, and unless she does, she cannot be at her best.

Negative Traits

Libras displaying the negative characteristics associated with their sign also tend to be:

- fearful

- lazy and indecisive

- manipulative

- know-it-all

- flirtatious

- narcissistic

- jealous

- depressed

Ask a Libra If…

Ask a Libra if you want to see both sides of a difficult or troublesome situation. Libras are notoriously good at being able to size up any situation and discover the pluses and minuses of it. Libra isn't merely content to analyze the available options, but actually believes that there are two sides to every story. Even if a Libra has a preference for one or the other, he will be fair in making an assessment.

Libras As Friends

Libras are loving friends and are unlikely to embarrass anyone with emotional outbursts. Libran friends are honest and treat their friends fairly. They need to keep a balance between work and play, and between their thoughts and their emotions. This is what makes them happy. Friends should never forget that the worst thing for a Libra is to be left alone for too long. If this happens, Libras can become irritable and depressed, and their self-esteem can suffer. Friends also need to know that Libras find it difficult to ask for help when they are feeling unhappy.

Sometimes Libras seem to have trouble making decisions, but this is because they must consider all sides of a question first. Libras can occasionally try the patience of their friends with their indecisiveness.

Libras are always striving for perfection, and need beauty and balance around them. The most important thing for a Libra person is the idea of harmony.

Looking for Love

Libras are very partner oriented and often find it difficult to function efficiently without one. It's not that they depend upon their partner for much. Libras need a partner so they can find out what they, themselves, think about something by bouncing it off of another person. When they find a partner who, in this way, enables them to feel the way they want to feel, they seek to make the partnership permanent. This often leads to partnerships that others have difficulty understanding. It also makes Libras very concerned with living up to the conditions of partnerships. Libras love to be in love.

Libras need good communication with others. The smooth-talking socialites of the zodiac, Libras are happy to flatter, to console, and to make their love interests feel comfortable. But that is not to say that they desire insincere flattery. They are extremely intelligent and can always tell if someone is being honest or merely trying to get on their good side. Libras want harmony above all else but will not be falsely placated just to achieve the semblance of it. They're also very considerate of a loved one's needs and always try to see things from their mate's point of view.

Even though Libras are not intellectual snobs, they do look for someone who is full of ideas and opinions and with whom they can have rousing discussions. There are times when even romantic infatuation or attraction isn't enough—Libra needs the words!

Finding That Special Someone

As Libras are extremely sociable, they have no problem meeting interesting people. Because their talent for conversation makes them interesting dinner party guests, they have more than their share of invitations. Since they have so many friends, it is not uncommon for Libras to be introduced to a potential love interest by mutual friends.

First Dates

A first date with a Libra usually involves some classy event where an attractive new outfit is required. Most Libras love the arts and parties. An ideal first date would be to any gathering where there was a mix of interesting people. Libras love good food but are often watching their weight, so the appetizers and wine served at such an event may be enough for them. Afterwards, though, they may choose to have a cup of coffee at a trendy place to discuss the evening's events. For Libra, the talk may even prove to be the best part of the date.

Libra in Love

The Libra can glow with love for the whole world when she meets the person of her dreams. She tends to fall in love with love itself and is eager to share life, with all its ups and downs, with her partner. The Libran ideal is a life that is filled with the gentle, peaceful, rosy glow of romance. She will do anything to avoid hurting her loved one, and can become extremely emotionally dependent on her partner.

Undying Love

The Libra is able to forgive a lot of his loved one's shortcomings. A loved one can lighten Libra's depressive moods with a genuine loving gesture. A Libra may argue or behave badly when he feels that something is unfair.

Libras are not nearly as high maintenance as they may appear. Because they are so reasonable, it is easy to talk to them about concerns in the relationship without them becoming aggravated or overly emotional. They are always willing to do their part in keeping the relationship not only working but improving.

Expectations in Love

The sign of Libra is one of the most positive for relationships, both romantic and committed partnerships of all kinds. If a Libra is in a relationship, he needs to be supported and cared for as well as admired and even exalted.

If a relationship is new, a Libra should make sure his partner is someone whom he likes a lot and who is willing to wait awhile before moving the relationship to the physical stage. When a Libra finds that person, you can rest assured that a wonderful time in his life is at hand and that his fabulous love life will be with someone positive whom he loves and trusts. Faithfulness and loyalty are essential to a Libra.

A Libra also needs a partner to have her own separate interests, as it is important to him to be free to get on with his work.

What Libras Look For

While Libras have a reputation for being attracted only to good-looking people, they are really looking for much more. They appreciate someone who is intelligent and has a pleasing personality. Most of all, they are dazzled by a person who can hold his own in conversational banter. While they are happiest when they can find someone who has all of these attributes, brains will always win out over looks with the clever people of this sign.

If Libras Only Knew

If Libras only knew that any trouble in a relationship with a Libra will come from one or both partners not fulfilling their obligations with honesty and a giving heart. Libra may have learned from others whom she looked up to and respected that this unequal and disappointing tendency was the way to act in a relationship. Libras believe deeply in the power of communication in any relationship. They feel that issues, good and bad, can be handled and solved as long as the talking doesn't stop.

Marriage

The person who partners Libra can expect the marriage to be happy and successful. Libra is the zodiac sign of partnerships, and typical Libras cannot imagine life without a relationship. A Libra will work hard and thoughtfully to make the partnership a harmonious balance of two personalities, but she needs plenty of encouragement.

The person who contemplates becoming the marriage partner of a typical Libra must realize that Libra forms partnerships to escape the loneliness that is always present inside her heart.

Libra wants a partner who has some good business or social connections, too. Libra has plenty of talent and energy and is ambitious to be successful in her marriage, business, and social life.

In a partnership, Libra generally takes charge of the financial planning, making sure that there is always a good bank balance.

Libra's Opposite Sign

The opposite sign of Libra is Aries. Although relationships between them can be difficult, they can also become extremely complementary. From Aries, Libra can learn to take the initiative and stand up for his beliefs. Libra can also learn from Aries how to become self-sufficient and how to gain a greater sense of personal identity, apart from his partner. In this way, Libra, the sign of partnership, may be able to enjoy a separate identity while in a partnership.

Pairing Up

In general, if people display the characteristics typical of their sign, intimate relationships between a Libra and another individual can be described as follows:

Libra with Libra

Harmonious; a meeting of minds, spirits, and hearts

Libra with Scorpio

Harmonious, if Scorpio can treat Libra with sensitivity

Libra with Sagittarius

Harmonious, since they are best friends as well as lovers

Libra with Capricorn
Difficult, because both signs are
stubborn

Libra with Aquarius
Harmonious; true soul mates forever

Libra with Pisces
Turbulent, unless Pisces can learn not
to lean on Libra

Libra with Aries
Difficult, yet each can learn a lot from
the other

Libra with Taurus
Turbulent, with a lot of bickering
and passion

Libra with Gemini
Harmonious; a joyful, fascinating
love match

Libra with Cancer
Difficult, yet enriched by shared values

Libra with Leo
Harmonious, since both partners are
equally romantic

Libra with Virgo
Harmonious, so long as financial
matters are handled with care

If Things Don't Work Out

Because of their dedication to a life partnership, Libras don't like to end a relationship. Not only is there the feeling of disappointment for a dream that has faded, but there is also the prospect of being alone. Libras are not happy alone, so ending a relationship takes a great deal of courage on their part. Thankfully, most of them have the good sense and self-confidence to prefer living solo to staying in a relationship that no longer works as a positive force in their life.

Libra at Work

Libras work very hard to attain the goal of resolving conflict, either through compromise and diplomacy or by fighting the good fight if they are forced to. They are constantly trying to balance the scales of justice regarding practically everything, and that can be very trying, not only personally but also for others. Their desire to make the perfect decision can sometimes prevent them from acting decisively until it is too late to do so. A Libra can be a bit bossy but uses charm and reasoning to convince people of the value of her side of an issue. Libras find it easy to associate and work with others. At work they can serve as good managers, counselors, and collaborators.

People often misread Libra's amiable personality for reticence or weakness, but this is not the case. Anyone who has ever gone up against Libra in a power play knows that she is not only determined but also extremely well versed in the art of arguing a point of view. Libras don't like being manipulated and are unlikely to stoop to this tactic themselves. But they do have the ability to defuse a challenger's argument with wit and charm. For the most part, they get along famously with others.

Typical Occupations

Libras are liable to be involved with any aspect of the law, politics, or diplomacy. Their eye for design may lead them into areas such as fashion, interior decoration, art dealership, and graphics. Naturally creative and artistic, some Libras are gifted fine artists, composers, and musicians. Others may find success as critics, writers, or managers in various areas of entertainment. They also enjoy working in jobs that involve talking and presentation, such as promotional work. Many Libras are good at planning business ventures. Finance is also a fair field, as Libras are trustworthy in handling other people's money.

In a profession or business, Libras often succeed as administrators, lawyers, doctors, antique dealers, or civil servants. Those with a gift for finance sometimes make good speculators, for they have the optimism and ability to recover from financial setbacks.

It is a good idea for a Libra to be doing work that involves interaction with the public or coworkers. Jobs that work best could involve publicity, negotiations, and working in the support industries that service weddings and parties.

Details, Details

When it comes to life's day-to-day details, Libras have the ability to handle them with ease. But that doesn't mean they always do. They sometimes overlook details, especially if they involve suffering or cannot be resolved elegantly. They need to fulfill their part of all agreements, rules, and regulations. A Libra must find a way that he can work with others without feeling that he has had to still his own unique voice to do it. Because this isn't always easy for him, he can become frustrated and unnecessarily argumentative. Similarly, working within time constraints or a budget can frazzle him and stifle his creative instincts.

In their continual search for balance, Libras strive to see both sides, even when that turns out to be an exercise in futility. Sometimes just for argument's sake they take an opposing viewpoint. This is their way of familiarizing themselves with all the possible details involved in a project or endeavor. But while it is important for a Libra to be acquainted with this information, he actually works much better as the "idea person," delegating the detail-oriented work to others.

Behavior and Abilities at Work

In the workplace, a typical Libra:

- ✿ is a great resource for ideas
- ✿ knows how to compromise
- ✿ likes to make contracts
- ✿ builds a good network of contacts
- ✿ takes time to do things properly
- ✿ looks for ways to advance her career

Libra As Employer

A typical Libra boss:

- doesn't like to be pushed too far

- is an extremely good analyst

- takes everyone's opinion into consideration

- suggests that she is an expert

- can argue both sides of an issue

- has a strong opinion about neatness

- is financially savvy

Libra As Employee

A typical Libra employee:

- makes good presentations
- has good manners
- is an effective mediator
- can be moody at times
- expects and gives a fair deal
- belongs to an organization
- needs a long vacation
- dresses well and appropriately

Libra As Coworker

Sometimes, fearful of discord, Libras become paralyzed with indecision. They easily see the value of another person's point of view. But often, if they do not hold a definite opinion of their own, they fail to take a stand. If they lose confidence in their own views and try to reconcile them with what others may think, they can become confused, vulnerable, and aggressive.

Money

If Libras are uncommunicative about any area of their life, that area is likely to be money. They usually handle their financial affairs with discretion, preferring to keep such things to themselves. It is also typical for Libras to refrain from telling people how much they spent for a particular item, since to them, it sounds like bragging.

Libras have the ability to be practical about money, but that doesn't mean that they always succeed. They have very extravagant tastes and can find it hard to live on a budget. Immediate gratification can be a problem for them, since when they see something beautiful they want to own it.

Beauty is as important to Libras as money, so if they are surrounded by beautiful things they count themselves wealthy. The best of them measure success by the harmonious elements working in their lives, not by how much money they have in the bank.

At Home

If an individual has the personality that is typical of those born with a Libra Sun sign, home is a place to retire to for rest and recuperation, to prepare for the next period of sustained activity.

Librans find home the one place where it is difficult for them to compromise. They simply have to have things their way, especially when it comes to their home's appearance, design, and decoration.

Behavior and Abilities at Home

Libra typically:

- uses good taste to make the decor beautiful

- offers good food and wines to guests

- keeps the home clean and tidy

- spends time just lounging around

- creates a healing environment

- makes a very gracious host

- takes an active role in redecorating

Leisure
Interests

A Libra loves a luxurious home where she can be totally lazy. While at rest, the Libran mind is rarely still, always planning ahead, and at times that is enough activity for her. She likes to have sensual bed linens and sophisticated colors surrounding her.

The typical Libra enjoys the following pastimes:

- listening to music
- reading poetry
- dancing classes
- spending time in romantic settings
- shopping for fashion
- gourmet cooking
- interior design as a hobby
- going to parties

Libra Likes

- getting flowers
- having friends around
- working with a partner
- well-made, expensive clothes
- a stimulating discussion
- planning a party
- having help
- attending to the finest details
- beautiful surroundings
- soft color schemes
- being admired

Libra Dislikes

- injustice
- disharmony
- sloppiness
- arguing in public
- ugly clothes
- having to make big decisions
- being alone
- bad manners
- taking out the garbage
- vulgarity

The Secret Side of Libra

Inside any Libra is a person who is terrified of being alone. The fear is usually well controlled, so the typical Libra always looks calm, collected, and in charge of any situation.

Good-natured and loving, Libras can also be petulant, and even objectionable, when asked to take orders. Similarly, they are extremely intelligent, yet sometimes gullible; they enjoy talking to people, yet can also be very attentive listeners. Although they believe in equality, they sometimes yearn to be subservient to their partners.

Venus ♀

Venus is the planet of romantic love, beauty, and the arts that are associated with them. Sociable Venus rules over parties and pleasurable meetings. She accomplishes her goals by attracting only what she wants and rejecting the rest, thus making taste and values two of her special talents. Diplomacy, tact, and gentleness are a few of the arts that are ruled by Venus.

The love and beauty that Venus represents have the power to both unite and heal, and a more desirable and powerful combination is difficult to imagine. Venus rules our senses of touch, taste, and smell—everything must achieve harmony before usefulness.

Bringing Up a Young Libra

Most young Libras learn quickly how to argue about everything with total conviction. At a very early age young Libra needs to be given direction and told, gently and firmly, what to do and when to do it. Little Libra uses this natural ability to make his needs and wants known. Parents needs to take an optimistic view of this tendency and should provide plenty of sound information. Young Libra absorbs information readily from books. What may appear to be reluctance to do something is often a sign that young Libra is giving extensive thought to the matter at hand.

While young Libras can pursue their interests alone, they also need company. It is from bonding with others that they learn who they really are. It is never a good idea to scold little Libras too much, especially in front of others. Doing so makes them feel ashamed and embarrassed. It could also make them feel that if they are going to fail, it had better not be in front of parents or other authority figures.

A harmonious environment and fair treatment are essential to the developing Libra. Privacy is regarded as sacred. Similarly, young Libra respects the privacy of others and keeps confidences. Affection is crucial.

Libra As a Parent

The typical Libra parent:

- ✹ tries to be just and fair
- ✹ may spoil the children
- ✹ shows much affection
- ✹ gives children the best possible education
- ✹ will probably dominate the family
- ✹ encourages artistic pursuits
- ✹ likes kids to be neat and well dressed
- ✹ stresses manners and good behavior
- ✹ encourages a child's fantasy life

The Libra Child

The typical Libra child:

* hates having to decide between two things

* does not like to be hurried

* has a naturally sweet temperament

* always seems mature for her age

* likes to be fair and to be treated fairly

* can charm her friends and parents

❀ obeys rules if they make sense

❀ loves bubble baths

❀ likes candy and desserts

❀ shares toys with other children

❀ is usually neat and clean

❀ is kindhearted

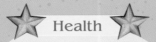

Health

Expecting a good life,
Libras easily become depressed
whenever difficulties arise and can
suffer from severe headaches in their
mental efforts to resolve problems.
When Libras are unhappy, they tend to
overeat. They are happier and healthier
when engaged in rewarding work. It can
also take a great deal of effort for
them to motivate themselves to
exercise regularly. Libras have
a generally strong

constitution, but their kidneys and bladder may let them down later in life due to their fondness for wining and dining.

Libra rules the adrenals, kidneys, skin, and lumbar nerves. Diseases such as kidney and bladder disorders, or eczema and skin diseases, can be a problem.

✦ Famous Libras ✦

Julie Andrews

Lorraine Bracco

Truman Capote

Catherine Deneuve

Michael Douglas

F. Scott Fitzgerald

George Gershwin

Rita Hayworth

Charlton Heston

Jesse Jackson

Ralph Lauren

John Lennon

Franz Liszt

Mickey Mantle

Eugene O'Neill

Gwyneth Paltrow

Luciano Pavarotti

Christopher Reeve

Anne Rice

Eleanor Roosevelt

Susan Sarandon

Paul Simon

Sting

Usher

Catherine Zeta-Jones

About the Authors

Internationally known self-help author Monte Farber's inspiring guidance and empathic insights impact everyone he encounters. Amy Zerner's exquisite one-of-a-kind spiritual couture creations and collaged fabric paintings exude her profound intuition and deep connection with archetypal stories and healing energies. Together, they have built The Enchanted World of Amy Zerner and Monte Farber: books, card decks, and

oracles that have helped millions discover their own spiritual paths.

Their best-selling titles include The Chakra Meditation Kit, The Enchanted Tarot, The Instant Tarot Reader, The Psychic Circle, Karma Cards, The Truth Fairy, The Healing Deck, True Love Tarot, Animal Powers Meditation Kit, The Breathe Easy Deck, The Pathfinder Psychic Talking Board, and Gifts of the Goddess Affirmation Cards.

For further information, please visit: **www.TheEnchantedWorld.com**